20 Forex Trading Strategies
(1 Hour Time Frame)

By Thomas Carter

Copyright © 2014 Thomas Carter
thomascarterbook.blogspot.com

All right reserved. No part of this book may be produced or transmitted in any form or by any means, electronic or mechanical, including photocopying, recording, or any information storage a nd retrieval system, without prior written permission of the author.

DISCLAIMER

Trading forex and other on-exchange and over-the-counter products carries a high level of risk and may not be suitable for all investors. The high degree of leverage associated with such trading can result in losses, as well as gains. the past performance of any trading strategy or methodology is not indicative of future results, which can vary due to market volatility; it should not be interpreted as a forecast of future performance You should carefully consider whether such trading is suitable for you in light of your financial condition, level of experience and appetite for risk and seek advice from independent financial adviser, if you have any doubts.

Table of Contents

DISCLAIMER..2
FOREX TRADING STRATEGY # 1..4
FOREX TRADING STRATEGY # 2..5
FOREX TRADING STRATEGY # 3..6
FOREX TRADING STRATEGY # 4..7
FOREX TRADING STRATEGY # 5..9
FOREX TRADING STRATEGY # 6..11
FOREX TRADING STRATEGY # 7..12
FOREX TRADING STRATEGY # 8..13
FOREX TRADING STRATEGY # 9..14
FOREX TRADING STRATEGY # 10..15
FOREX TRADING STRATEGY # 11..16
FOREX TRADING STRATEGY # 12..17
FOREX TRADING STRATEGY # 13..18
FOREX TRADING STRATEGY # 14..19
FOREX TRADING STRATEGY # 15..20
FOREX TRADING STRATEGY # 16..22
FOREX TRADING STRATEGY # 17..23
FOREX TRADING STRATEGY # 18..24
FOREX TRADING STRATEGY # 19..25
FOREX TRADING STRATEGY # 20..26
FINAL WORDS..27

FOREX TRADING STRATEGY # 1

Currency: EUR/USD

Time Frame: 1 Hour

Indicators:
SMA 3
EMA 50
Full Stochs (50, 60, 30) with an EMA 8 attached.
MACD (65, 75, 35) with an EMA 8 attached.

Stop Loss: 50 pips

Take Profit: 100 pips

LONG => Enter a trade when SMA 3 have crossed and above EMA 50 AND Full Stochs OR MACD have crossed their EMA 8. You don't have to wait for the MACD or Stochs to cross their own signal line, just crossing their EMA 8 is enough, but never enter a trade before the SMA 3 and EMA 50 have crossed too!

SHORT => Enter a trade when SMA 3 have crossed and below EMA 50 AND Full Stochs OR MACD have crossed their EMA 8. You don't have to wait for the MACD or Stochs to cross their own signal line, just crossing their EMA 8 is enough, but never enter a trade before the SMA 3 and EMA 50 have crossed too!

FOREX TRADING STRATEGY # 2

Currency: GBP/USD

Time Frame: 1 Hour

Indicators:
SMA 9
SMA 100

Method
LONG - When the 9 SMA crosses above the 100 SMA
SHORT - When the 9 SMA crosses below the 100 SMA

Stop Loss: 50 pips

Target: 100 pips or close your position when the 9 SMA crosses the 100 SMA in reverse (9 SMA below 100 SMA for long and 9 SMA above 100 SMA for short).

FOREX TRADING STRATEGY # 3

Currency: EUR/USD

Time Frame: 1 Hour

Indicators:
EMA 6
EMA 23
Stochastic (5,3,3)
MACD (30,60,30)

Method:
LONG – EMA 6 crosses above EMA 23, MACD indicates an uptrend, stochastic crosses upward, buy as close to the 6 EMA as possible.

SHORT – EMA 6 crosses below EMA 23, MACD indicates a downtrend, stochastic crosses downward, sell as close to the 6 EMA as possible.

Stop Loss: 20 - 30 pips

Target: 50 - 60 pips

FOREX TRADING STRATEGY # 4

Currency: EUR/USD or GBP/USD

Time Frame: 1 Hour

Indicators:
Heiken Ashi (make it white for bullish candle and red for bearish candle)
14 SMA
OSMA (12,26,9)
10 period Momentum – level set at 100
RSI (5)

Long Entry Rules:
1. A bullish Heiken Ashi candle (white) crosses above the 14 SMA.
2. The OsMA crosses above its Zero level.
3. The Momentum indicator crosses above the 100 level.
4. The RSI crosses above the 50 level.
5. As soon as all conditions mentioned above are met, we wait for the current candle to
close then place a buy order at market.
6. Set the Stop Loss a few pips below the last swing low point.
7. Set the Take Profit at double the amount of the Stop loss.
8. We can close our long trade without waiting for the Take profit to be hit when OsMA
crosses below the Zero level.

Short Entry Rules:
1. A bearish Heiken Ashi candle (red) crosses below the 14 SMA.
2. The OsMA moves below the Zero level.
3. The Momentum indicator crosses below the 100 level.
4. The RSI crosses under the 50 level.
5. As soon as all conditions mentioned above are met, wait for the current candle to

close and open a short trade.
6. Set the Stop Loss a few pips above the last swing high.
7. Set the Take Profit at double the amount of the Stop loss.
8. We can close our short trade without waiting for the Take profit to be hit when OsMA
goes above the Zero level.

FOREX TRADING STRATEGY # 5

Currency: EUR/USD or GBP/USD

Time Frame: 1 Hour

Indicators:
- 55 Smoothed Moving Average (SMMA) - set to High price.
- 55 Smoothed Moving Average (SMMA) - set to Low price.
- 55 period Williams' Percent Range (%R) - levels set at -25 and -75 values.
- Stochastic Oscillator - %K period = 5, Slowing = 5, %D period = 5, Price field =
Low/High, MA method = Simple, with levels at 20 and 80 (default).

Long Entry:
1. Price must cross above the 55 SMMA set to High (Green).
2. The %R crosses above the -25 level.
3. The Stochastic Oscillator is above its Signal line.
4. When all the conditions mentioned above are met, we can place our long position.
We have two possible entry types: Aggressive and Conservative.
In the Aggressive entry, we open a buy order without waiting for the signal candle to close.
In the Conservative entry, we wait for the signal candle to close above the 55 SMMA set to High before placing our trade. This serves as a confirmation that we are trading on the right side of the market.
5. Set the Stop Loss a few pips below the most recent swing low point.
6. Set the Take Profit level twice the amount of the stop loss, or close the trade when
the price closes below the 55 SMMA set to High.

Short Entry:

1. Price must cross below the 55 SMMA set to Low (Crimson).
2. The %R crosses below the -75 level.
3. The Stochastic Oscillator is below its Signal line.
4. When all the conditions mentioned above are met, we can open a short position.

For an Aggressive entry, we don't need to wait for the current candle to close before entering the trade.

For a Conservative entry, wait for the candle to close below the 55 SMMA set to Low before placing the trade.

5. Set the Stop Loss a few pips above the most recent swing high point.
6. Set the Take Profit twice the amount of the Stop Loss, or close the trade when the
price closes above the 55 SMMA set to Low.

FOREX TRADING STRATEGY # 6

Currency: EUR/USD or GBP/USD

Time Frame: 1 Hour

Indicators:
EMA 5
EMA 15
EMA 60

Long Trade Rules:
We must first establish that we're in a strong uptrend using these 3 rules:
1. EMA 60 and EMA15 are both pointing up.
2. EMA5 is above EMA15.
3. EMA15 is above EMA60.

When we have these three conditions, we know that we're in an uptrend. We then wait for the price to fall back, and touch the EMA60. When that happens, we enter the trade.
Stop Loss = 30 pips
Target Profit = 50 pips

Short Trade Rules:
We must first establish that we're in a strong downtrend using these 3 rules:
1. EMA60 and EMA15 are both pointing down.
2. EMA5 is below EMA15.
3. EMA15 is below EMA60.

When we have these three conditions, we know that we're in a downtrend. We then wait for the price to retrace, and touch the EMA60. When that happens, we enter the trade.
Stop Loss = 30 pips
Target = 50 pips

FOREX TRADING STRATEGY # 7

Currency: EUR/USD

Time Frame: 1 Hour

Indicators:
EMA 80
EMA 21
EMA 13
EMA 5
EMA 3
RSI (21)

Long Trade Rules:
–3 EMA crosses 5 EMA upward in a uptrend market
–Both 3 EMA and 5 EMA cross the 13 EMA and 21 EMA
–RSI is above 50
–Both EMA 13 and EMA 21 are above EMA 80
Stop Loss = 20 – 30 pip
Exit when 3 EMA crosses below 5 EMA or RSI < 50

Short Trade Rules:
–3 EMA crosses 5 EMA downward in downtrend market
–Both 3 EMA and 5 EMA cross the 13 EMA and 21 EMA
–RSI is below 50
–Both EMA 13 and EMA 21 are below EMA 80
Stop Loss = 20 – 30 pips
Exit when 3 EMA crosses above 5 EMA or RSI > 50

FOREX TRADING STRATEGY # 8

Currency: EUR/USD or GBP/USD

Time Frame: 1 Hour

Indicators:
Bollinger Band (20,3)
3 EMA
MACD (6,17,1)
RSI (14)

Long Entry Rules:
1. The 3 period EMA must cross above the Middle Bollinger Band.
2. The MACD must cross above the 0 level.
3. The 14 period RSI must cross above the 50 level.
4. When all the conditions above are met, place a buy order at market.
5. Set the Stop Loss a few pips below the nearest swing low or the Lower Bollinger Band, whichever is closer.
6. Set the Take Profit at the Upper Bollinger Band or use a fixed profit = 50 pips

Short Entry Rules:
1. The 3 period EMA must cross under the Middle Bollinger Band.
2. The MACD must fall below the 0 level.
3. The 14 period RSI must move below the 50 level.
4. When all the conditions above are met, place a sell order.
5. Set the Stop Loss a few pips above the nearest swing high or the Upper Bollinger Band, whichever is closer.
6. Set the Take Profit at the Lower Bollinger Band or a fixed target = 50 pips

FOREX TRADING STRATEGY # 9

Currency: EUR/USD

Time Frame: 1 Hour

Indicatos:
SAR – step 0.1, maximum 0.2
EMA 5
EMA 12
EMA 34

LONG ENTRY:
EMA5 > EMA12 > EMA 34 and Last SAR is ABOVE Current SAR and Current SAR is UNDER EMA5

SHORT ENTRY:
EMA5 < EMA12 < EMA 34 and Last SAR is UNDER Current SAR and Current SAR is ABOVE EMA5
Stop Loss = 30 pip
Target = 50 pips

FOREX TRADING STRATEGY # 10

Currency: EUR/USD

Time Frame: 1 Hour

Indicators:
EMA 14 applied to high
EMA 14 applied to low
Parabolic SAR (step 0.02, 0.2)

Methods:
LONG - place a buy order when price closes above the 14 high and PSAR is under the candle
SHORT - place a sell order when price closes below the 14 low and PSAR is above the candle.
Stop Loss = 50-60 pips
Target Profit = 60-100 pips

FOREX TRADING STRATEGY # 11

Currency: EUR/USD

Time Frame: 1 Hour

Indicators:
5 EMA shift 5
75 EMA
Bollinger Band (20,2)
RSI (14)

Methods:
LONG - When a candle closes above the 75 ema as well as the bollinger middle line, and the RSI line breaks above the 50 line, Stop Loss => place stop 2 pips below whichever is the middle of the 75ema, high of the signal candle, and swing high of the 5ema.
Target Profit => same as the stop loss or double the stop loss
SHORT - When a candle closes below the 75 ema as well as the bollinger middle line, and the RSI line breaks below the 50 line
Stop Loss - place stop 2 pips + the spread above whichever is the middle of the 75ema, high of the signal candle, and swing high of the 5ema.
Target Profit => same as the stop loss or double the stop loss

FOREX TRADING STRATEGY # 12

Currency: EUR/USD or GBP/USD

Indicators:
- 3 EMA (Exponential Moving Average) set to the close price.
- 5 EMA (Exponential Moving Average) set to the open price.
- 34 EMA (Exponential Moving Average) set to the close price.
- 89 EMA (Exponential Moving Average) set to the close price.
- 3 RSI (Relative Strength Index) with levels at 20 and 80.
- Stochastic (5,3,3) with default settings and levels at 20 and 80.
- 14 ADX (Average Directional Movement Index) with +D and –D line only.

Long Entry Rules:
- The 34 EMA must be above the 89 EMA.
- The 3 RSI must cross above the 80 level.
- The Stochastic must be above its Signal line.
- The +D ADX line must be above the –D line.
- The 3 EMA must cross above the 5 EMA.
- When all the rules mentioned above are met, in whatever order, we can open a buy trade.
Stop Loss => below the 34 EMA or the last swing low point.
Target Profit => double the amount of the stop loss.

Short Entry Rules:
- 34 EMA must be below the 89 EMA
- The 3 RSI must cross under the 20 level
- The stochastic must be below its signal line
- The -D ADX lines must be above the +D line
- The 3 EMA must cross under the 5 EMA
- When all the rules mentioned above are met, regardless of the sequence, we can open a sell order.
Stop Loss => above the 34 EMA or the last swing high point.
Target Profit => double the amount of the stop loss.

FOREX TRADING STRATEGY # 13

Currency: EUR/USD or GBP/USD

Time Frame: 1 Hour

Indicators:
5 EMA -- YELLOW
10 EMA -- RED
RSI (10 - Apply to Median Price: HL/2) -- One level at 50.

Method:
Enter LONG when the Yellow EMA crosses the Red EMA from underneath.
RSI must be approaching 50 from the BOTTOM and cross 50 to warrant entry.

Enter SHORT when the Yellow EMA crosses the Red EMA from the top.
RSI must be approaching 50 from the TOP and cross 50 to warrant entry.
Stop Loss = 30 pips
Target Profit = 50 pips

FOREX TRADING STRATEGY # 14

Currency: EUR/USD

Time Frame: 1 Hour

Indicators:
EMA 5
EMA 13
EMA 62
MACD (30,60,30)

Long Rules:
–5 EMA is above 13 EMA
–13 EMA is above 62 EMA
–MACD is uptrend (above 0 line)
–When all conditions are met and 13 EMA is at least 30-40 pip away from 62 EMA get ready to enter the trade.

Short Rules:
–5 EMA is below 13 EMA
–13 EMA is below 62 EMA
–MACD is downtrend (below 0 line)
–When all conditions are met and 13 EMA is at least 30-40 pip away from 62 EMA get ready to enter the trade.
Stop Loss = 30 pips
Target Profit = 50 pips

FOREX TRADING STRATEGY # 15

Currency: EUR/USD or GBP/USD

Time Frame: 1 Hour

Indicators:
–EMA 5
–EMA 21
–RSI (21)
–Candlestick Pattern: Bullish Engulfing, Bearish Engulfing, Hammer, Inverted Hammer

Long Trade Rules:
–EMA 5 crosses EMA 21 to the upside
–RSI (21) > 50
–Bullish Engulfing or Hammer candlestick pattern

Short Trade Rules:
–EMA 5 crosses EMA 21 to the downside
–RSI (21) < 50
–Bearish Engulfing or Inverted Hammer candlestick pattern.

Stop Loss: recent swing low

Exit Rules for Long Trades:
- Exit the trade when EMA 5 crosses back below EMA 12 Or RSI 21 < 50.
- Or when price stalls at major resistance, trend line, pivot points, Fibonacci projection target.
- Or when bearish engulfing patterns or inverted hammer patterns form.

Exit Rules for Short Trades:

-Exit our short trade when EMA 5 crosses above EMA 12 Or RSI 21 > 50
- Or when price stalls at major support, trend line, pivot points, Fibonacci projection target.
- Or when bullish engulfing patterns or hammer patterns form.
- Or double the stop loss

FOREX TRADING STRATEGY # 16

Currency: EUR/USD or GBP/USD

Time Frame: 1H, 30m, 15m, 5m

Indicators:
Just candlestick

Long Entry:
- Wait for a current hour candle to close
- If all 4 of the last candles (M5, M15, M30 and 1H) closed in "green" – wait
for the price to go another 3 pips above the close and instantly place a BUY
order.

Short Entry:
- Wait for a current hour candle to close
- If all 4 last candles (M5, M15, M30 and 1H) closed in "red" – wait for the
price to go another 3 pips below the close and instantly place a SELL order.
Stop Loss = 20 pips
Take Profit = 30 – 40 pips

FOREX TRADING STRATEGY # 17

Currency: EUR/USD

Time Frame: 1 Hour

Indicators:
100 EMA
28 Smooth Moving Average
MACD (30,60,30)

Long Entry:
- 28 Smooth Moving Average crosses 100 EMA upside
- MACD is uptrend (above 0 line)

Short Entry:
- 28 Smooth Moving Average crosses 100 WMA downside
- MACD is downtrend (below 0 line)
Stop Loss = 50 pips
Target Profit = 70 - 100 pips

FOREX TRADING STRATEGY # 18

Currency: EUR/USD or GBP/USD

Time Frame: 1 Hour

Indicators:
5 EMA
10 EMA
Stochastic (14,3,3)
RSI (14)

Long Rules:
Buy when 5 EMA crosses above 10 EMA and Stochastic lines are heading north (up) and Stochastic is not in overbought position (above 80.00 level) and RSI is above 50.

Short Rules:
Sell when 5 EMA crosses below 10 EMA and Stochastic lines are heading south (down) and Stochastic is not in oversold position (below 20.00 level), and RSI is below 50.
Stop Loss: recent swing low / high
Take profit: same as stop loss or twice the stop loss

FOREX TRADING STRATEGY # 19

Currency: EUR/USD or GBP/USD

Time Frame: 1 Hour

Indicators:
- Parabolic SAR (0.02,0.2)
  - ADX (50) with +D and -D lines

Long Entry:
Buy when the +DI line is above the -DI line, and Parabolic SAR gives buy signal (Parabolic SAR is below candle).

Short Entry:
Sell when the +DI line is below the -DI line, and Parabolic SAR gives sell signal (Parabolic SAR is above candle).
Stop Loss = 50 pips
Target Profit = 50 pips or when +D line and -D line have crossed again.

FOREX TRADING STRATEGY # 20

Currency: EUR/USD

Time Frame: 1 Hour

Indicators:
- 18 EMA & 28 EMA (red color)
- 5 WMA (blue) & 12 WMA (yellow)
- RSI (21)
WMA = Weight Moving Average

Entry Signal:
You should only open a position, when the red tunnel is extremely narrow or crossed !

Long Entry:
- 5 WMA & 12 WMA cross the red tunnel upwards. (If the 5 WMA also crosses the 12 WMA upwards, then the signal is extra strong).
- RSI >50

Short Entry:
- 5 WMA & 12 WMA cross the red tunnel downwards. (If the 5 WMA also crosses the 12 WMA downwards, then the signal is extra strong).
- RSI<50

Stop Loss = 50 pips

Take Profit = 5o pips or 5 WMA and 12 WMA have crossed again.

FINAL WORDS

Thank you for purchasing this book. I hope this book was able to help you to jump start your forex trading adventure. If you enjoyed this book, please take the time to share your thoughts and post a review on amazon. It's be greatly appreciated !

I wish you all the best with trading,

Thomas Carter